TIGER LILIES
AND
OTHER BEASTLY PLANTS

by

Elizabeth Ring

Illustrated by Barbara Bash

WALKER AND COMPANY
NEW YORK

Thanks to —

Brooklyn Botanical Garden Library
New York Botanical Garden Library
Denver Botanic Gardens
Maria Mitchell Natural History Library, Nantucket Island
Smithsonian Institution Botanical Library, Washington, D.C.

Library of Congress Cataloging in Publication Data

Ring, Elizabeth, 1920-
  Tiger lilies and other beastly plants.

  Includes index.
  Summary: Describes several plants that remind us in some way of
animals, including the foxglove, pussy willow, skunk cabbage, and
snapdragon.
  1. Plants—Juvenile literature. [1. Plants.   2. Plant names,
Popular.   3. Animals—Miscellanea]   I. Bash, Barbara, ill.   II. Title.
QK49.R55   1984   582.13   84-7499
ISBN 0-8027-6540-8

First published in the United States of America
in 1984 by the Walker Publishing Company, Inc.

Published simultaneously in Canada by John Wiley & Sons
Canada, Limited, Rexdale, Ontario.

ISBN: 0-8027-6540-8
Library of Congress Catalog Number:
Printed in the United States of America
10   9   8   7   6   5   4   3   2   1

Printed in Hong Kong by South China Printing Company.

For Kendel, Jenny and Jack

CONTENTS

Tiger Lily 6
Pussy Willow 8
Elephant's Ear 10
Skunk Cabbage 12
Snapdragon 14
Horsetail 16
Mouse-ear 18
Snake Gourd 20
Foxglove 22
Moth Mullein 24
Snail Flower 26
Spider Lily 28
Glossary 30
Plant Index 32

All spring and summer, strange "animals" abound in the woods, fields, swamps and gardens.

Some are enormous; some are tiny. Some look wild and fierce; some look gentle and sweet. Some smell wonderful; some have a terrible smell.

When you're out for a walk, keep an eye peeled. You'll meet "tigers" and "snakes," little white "mice," and a host of other "beastly" creatures.

They are all plants. They have leaves or stalks or flowers that remind you, somehow, of animals — or parts of animals: noses, tails, paws, wings. It may be something in their shapes or their colors. Or it might be the way they "behave."

There's a real "menagerie" out there — growing out of the ground, not waiting to pounce but to be found.

Wild "tigers" are galloping through the field. They are down by the stream, too, and along the road. Their shiny orange heads lift in the summer breeze.

These tigers are different from the orange tiger at the zoo. It has black stripes and it growls. These tigers are orange too but they have colored spots instead of stripes and they never make a sound. They are tiger lilies — so called for their tiger-like colors.

Tiger lilies were once kept in gardens, just as the tiger is kept in the zoo. But the tiger lilies escaped. They spread fast — in wet and dry ground, in sun and shade. (They grow *best* in light, rich soil that isn't too wet.)

You can't miss them. Their bright, shiny flowers stand high in a field.

Up close, you can see that the six, spotted petals turn back from the flower's deep center. The whole flower looks like a Turkish hat. *Stamens* poke out from the flower's center. They look like little pickaxes on long, bending handles. The long, seed-bearing part in the middle is the *pistil.*

It's no wonder tiger lilies spread fast. New plants can start in so many ways. Lilies may grow from seeds. They also grow from white bulbs. The bulbs stay in the ground all winter and send up stems in the spring. New plants also come from "bulbils" (little black bulbs that grow at the base of the leaves). The bulbils drop from the stems and root themselves.

In the spring, when snow is still on the ground, hundreds of silver-gray "pussies" show up on the red-brown branches of willows down by the pond.

Touch them. When you rub upwards, their "fur" feels silky and smooth. Rub down, and the fur feels fuzzy and rough. It feels just like real kitten's fur, smoothed head to tail or roughed tail to head.

The pussies or *catkins* have burst out of the nut-shaped buds along the branches. Very soon, the catkins will open and you will see that they are made up of tiny flowers.

Some plants will have bright orange or yellow flowers. These are male flowers carrying yellow pollen. Touch the pollen; yellow dust will stick to your fingers.

Other plants will have light green flowers. Insects visit the plants and carry the pollen from flower to flower. The green flowering plants are female. The pollen will help them make seeds that will grow into new plants.

If you cut some willow branches in the spring before the catkins flower the "pussies" will stay with you all year long.

PUSSY WILLOW
Salix discolor

The "elephants" are all ears. They have no long, swaying trunks or log-shaped legs. Only ears. The ears turn slowly as the air whispers by. They look as if they're listening, but, of course, they can't hear a thing. They are the leaves of the elephant's-ear plants.

The leaves grow two and even three feet long, often touching the ground. Each leaf is as wide as a knight's shield. You can easily hide behind a big, thick, green "ear."

The tiny flowers of an elephant's-ear plant hide, too. They're almost lost among the huge leaves.

Elephant's ears grow from starchy *tubers.* In the South Pacific Islands and in some southern states, the tubers of certain elephant's ear plants are grown as food. These *edible* (eatable) plants are called "taro" or "eddo" or "dasheen," depending on where they grow.

In Hawaii, taro roots are steamed, peeled, mashed, mixed with water and strained to make "poi," a famous and deliciously sticky Hawaiian dish.

The elephant's-ear tubers are *never* eaten raw. The raw tubers contain sharp crystals — like slivers of glass. The slivers would cut your mouth. Cooking, however, destroys the dangerous glassy bits.

If you'd like to grow big, beautiful elephant's ears — to enjoy, not to eat — just plant some tubers in good, rich soil. Beside a pool is a good place. In about seven months you'll have something to whisper to or hide behind — or just to look at as the giant ears turn slowly this way and that.

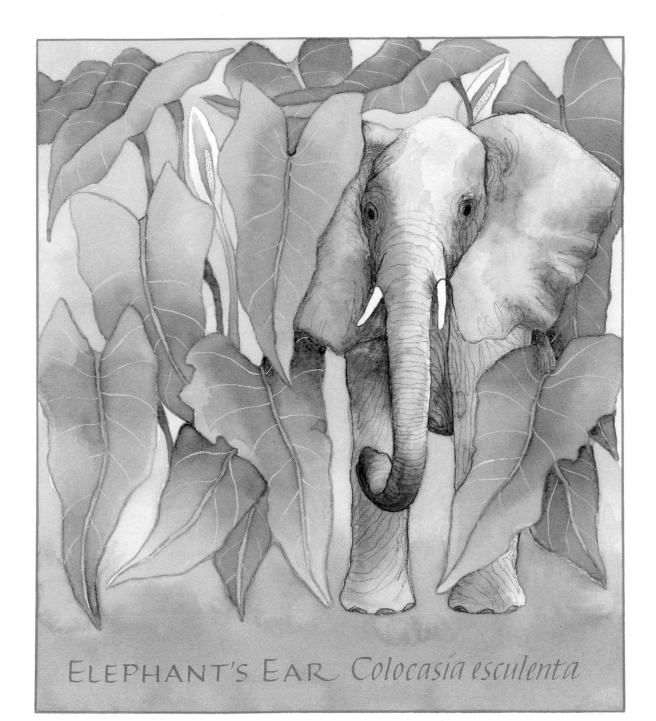

ELEPHANT'S EAR *Colocasia esculenta*

You can tell by the smell when "skunks" are around! They arrive in the spring — even before pussy willows do.

They poke their heads up from the wet, cold ground. Their heads are not black and white, like skunks' heads. First, all you can see is something purplish and round in the mud. Later, green leaves uncurl. But even before the leaves come, the smell announces: it's skunk cabbage time!

The skunk cabbage smell comes from all parts of the plant. It's in the tiny, hidden flowers and berries. It's in the purple-and-green-spotted leafy part that hides the flowers. It's in the cabbagelike leaves — especially if they're crushed. Then you really have to hold your nose!

The smell is useful to the plant because it attracts insects that carry pollen from one skunk cabbage to another. The tiny grains of pollen help to form *seeds* so that new skunk cabbage plants grow.

The leaves of the skunk cabbage plants grow tall. They look like cabbage leaves. These strong, smelly leaves attract many creatures besides insects. Lizards live beneath the leaves. Birds build nests among them. The skunky smell protects them — just as a skunk's smell keeps a skunk's enemies away — by smelling like a skunk!

SKUNK CABBAGE

Symplocarpus foetidus

It's summer and "dragons" have burst into the garden: purple ones, red ones, white ones, yellow ones, two-toned and striped ones. They have long, handsome snouts. They pout. But no flames shoot from their mouths. They are snapdragon flowers.

Snapdragons are so tame you can play games with them. Squeeze their throats gently and their mouths fly open. Let go and their mouths shut. The snapdragon will snap at your nose — but it won't hurt.

Snapdragons *do* "swallow" bumble bees alive. Almost. The bee lands on the flower's fat lower lip. The bee's weight pulls the lower lip away from the upper lip. The bee then crawls inside, head first. All you can see of the bee is its round, furry rear end. The whole flower trembles and sags: the bee is busy searching deep down for sweet nectar. Pretty soon the bee backs out and buzzes off. The snapdragon's mouth shuts again. Few other insects are heavy enough to open the flower's lips.

A butterly lights. It's not nearly heavy enough to part the snapdragon's lips. Instead, it slips its long sipping-tube between the two lips and pokes down to the nectar. Not many other insects have such long "straws."

Both bees and butterflies carry pollen from flower to flower, helping seeds form.

The next time you find your lower lip stuck out in a pout, look in the mirror. What kind of face is that — a dragon's? Or maybe it's more like a lion's? Or a calf's? "Lion's mouth" and "calf's snout" are a few of the other names for the plant best known as "snapdragon."

SNAPDRAGON
Antirrhinum majus

On an August day, when it's too warm to race and chase, you'll see "horses" standing stock-still in the meadow. When the wind plays, the horses' "tails" flick friskily.

More horses march along roadsides and sandbanks. They trot beside railroad tracks and across other stony places. You'll find them in marshes, too. They cause lots of trouble in gardens. They are horsetail weeds, and they're everywhere.

Horsetail plants grow two sets of stalks each year. The first stalks grow in the spring. They are tall, straight and knobby. They look like skinny, tan-colored asparagus stalks. New stalks grow in the summer. Long, brush-like branches spring from these stalks. To some people they look like horses' tails and this has given them their name.

Some April day, find an "asparagus-stalk" horsetail. Run your hand lightly up the rough stem. Does it feel like sandpaper? The stalks contain *silica.* That's the same fine grain found in sandpaper and some cleansing powders. One kind of horsetail has so much silica it's called "scouring rush." Two or three hundred years ago, pioneers used scouring rush stems as scrub brushes to clean pots and pans and to polish wood and metal. When you go camping, you could use horsetails to clean off your plate.

Break off one of these stalks. You'll find it is hollow, like a pipe. The stem grows in sections, like tinker-toy parts fitted together. Pull them apart and they go pop.

The small, black *scales* at the joints are too small to be called leaves, but they are like leaves. The yellow knob at the top of the stalk holds thousands of tiny green *spores.* When the spores are ripe they will burst from the knob and be scattered by wind and water. Some will sprout and make new horsetail plants.

Millions of years ago, horsetails grew sixty feet tall, like trees. The horsetails you see today are living fossils of those giants of old.

HORSETAIL
Equisetum Hyemale

W atch where you step as you cross the lawn. There's a "mouse!" There's another. And another. Tiny ears twitch as you go by. The mice won't run away. They are mouse-ear plants.

You'll find wild "mouse ears" in fields, woods, and along roadsides. They like to live in wet places, but they settle in dry places too. When they scatter themselves in lawns and gardens mouse-ears bother people. That's because their tough roots are very hard to dig up. Some people *like* some kinds of mouse-ears because they look pretty in gardens.

Pick a mouse-ear plant. Feel the furry leaves and stem? Now, close your eyes and imagine you are holding a small mouse!

Each flower has five notched petals. (You might find a blossom with only four petals, but hardly ever; they are as scarce as four-leaf clovers.)

Mouse-ears grow from seeds. Small *capsules* hold the seeds until they are ripe, in September or October. Then the capsules open, and the seeds scatter — all over the place. Mouse-ear plants multiply in a big way — like mice!

Mouse-ears have many cousins. They all belong to one family called "chickweed." Chickens love to eat chickweed, and that's how the family name came about. This is probably the first time you've heard of a chicken eating a mouse's ear!

MOUSE·EAR
Cerastium vulgatum

Slender green "snakes" lurk high in the trees in hot tropical places. When the wind blows, the snakes' bodies twist and writhe. These snakes won't flick out their tongues at you or wrap you up in their coils. They are snake *gourds*.

The gourds are the fruit of a tall-growing vine. In parts of Asia and Australia, wild snake gourds grow to be six feet long. Then they look like green pythons, or — less scary — like huge, crooked cucumbers.

Gourds belong to the same plant family as cucumbers, squashes and melons, which we eat. We rarely eat gourds. Instead, we hollow them out and use them as ornaments, perhaps piled in a bowl on the living room table. Or we cut hollowed gourds in half and use them as saucers, cups and bowls.

In India and other countries of the Far East, however, snake gourds are eaten. The gourds are picked when they are young. Then they are sliced and boiled, the same way squashes are cooked.

You can grow snake gourds by planting seeds indoors under glass. When the weather is warm enough, put them out in the ground. Vines will climb high on a fence. All summer you can watch the gourds grow and the white, fringed, cup-shaped flowers bloom. If you were to tie weights to the ends of the gourds they'd grow straight. Then they'd look more like baseball bats than snakes. Sometimes, in fact, snake gourds are called "club gourds."

Snake gourds are *annual* plants; that is, they last only one year and then die. So you'll have to start all over again each spring — planting seeds, transplanting plants — to keep your garden alive with "snakes."

SNAKE GOURD
Trichosanthes cucumeroides

Can you imagine a fox wearing gloves? Not easily. Yet, look! Foxgloves are out there in the back yard. They are strewn all over the fields and in clearings in the woods too. They are foxglove flowers.

Watch for them in May. They'll be around through September. Most often you see purple blossoms, but some flowers are rose, or pink, or white, or yellow or blue. They grow in *racemes,* bunched along a long stem. Some plants have as many as eighty flowers on one stalk.

Pick five foxglove flowers. Slip the little tubes on the ends of your fingers. It's something like wearing the fingertips snipped from a velvet-soft glove.

Look inside a bell-shaped blossom. See the spots on the lower lip? Now stand aside for a while. Most likely you'll see a bumble bee alight — right on the spots. The bee will probably follow the spotted trail into the flower. The spots are sometimes called the "honey line," because they lead to the sweet *nectar* deep inside the open flower.

When the bee leaves, you can bet it'll carry pollen away. When the pollen reaches another foxglove flower, seeds will be able to grow. Then, when the seeds are ripe, they'll be scattered by the wind. Some seeds are planted in gardens.

Foxgloves help people. A special chemical called *digitalis* is in the plant's long, hairy leaves. The chemical is used to make a medicine that is good for certain kinds of heart disease.

Unfortunately, foxgloves can hurt people too. Whoever eats any part of the plant can be poisoned. In fact, foxgloves are sometimes called "dead men's bells."

If you find it hard to imagine a fox wearing gloves, try thinking of the flowers as "folks' gloves." The plant goes by that name, too. But mostly you hear "foxgloves," so stretch your imagination enough to picture a fox with gloves on its paws!

FOXGLOVE
Digitalis purpurea

All summer "moths" ride softly on the gentle air. You see them soaring by roadsides, over bare, stony places. They rest half-hidden in meadow grasses. They are moth mullein weeds.

The yellow or white flowers flutter around tall, slender stems.

The five glowing petals of each flower open wide, like moths' wings. Touch a petal. It feels soft as a moth. Touch a green leaf. It, too, is smooth and velvety. The word "mullein" means "soft."

See the lavender-haired *stamens* at the center of the flower? Do they look like a moth's antennae?

Watch to see if butterflies visit the moth mullein during the day. Notice if moths fly to it in the evening or at night. Some people say these insects are attracted to the weed for its nectar. If butterflies and moths do stop by, their visit probably carries pollen from one flower to another, helping the plants make more moth mullein weeds.

MOTH MULLEIN *Verbascum blattaria*

Dozens of "snails" cling silently to vines on the garden wall. These snails simply sit; they do not inch along. They have no sticky, flat pad-feet that snails usually travel on. They have no hard shells to hide in. They are snail flowers.

Just before they come into bloom the coiled flowers look like real snail shells — except that they are yellow or white, with pale purple wings and soft, sweet-smelling petals. A real snail never smelled so nice!

Several snail flowers crowd on the sides of a flower stalk, or *peduncle,* like barnacles clustered on rocks. Choose one snail flower and count its coils. Each usually has four or five rings.

Snail flower vines are as strong as bean stalks. And no wonder: The plants are part of the bean family that includes string beans and limas.

In warm places, like Southern California, the twining snail flower vines grow to be ten or twelve feet long. They swarm over hedges and trees — sometimes smothering them. As you may imagine, they can be a great nuisance.

But they are beautiful — wherever they grow. In cool climates snail flowers are started in warm greenhouses. In the summer they can be planted in gardens.

Long *pods* grow on the vine, too. They are shaped like string beans. The pods hold little brown seeds. When the seeds are ripe, some of them will scatter and start new snail flower plants.

If snail flowers look to you more like corkscrews than snails — go ahead, call them "corkscrew flowers." Lots of other people do.

SNAIL FLOWER
Phaseolus caracalla

Big white "spiders" dangle long, skinny "legs" by the garden wall. But these airy danglers will never weave a web, catch a fly or crawl up your arm. They are spider lilies.

A real spider has eight legs. Spider lilies have only six "legs": three long, thin white *petals* and three white *sepals,* the parts just outside of the petals. In this plant they look just like the petals. As the pale blossoms are stirred by the air, the lilies wiggle and wave — in a very spidery way.

Look at the bottom of a spider lily flower. The petals and sepals together form a small cup. In the center of the cup is a tiny crown made of white tissue that looks something like bandage gauze. The flower's six pollen-bearing stamens spring up from the crown, and a long, seed-making pistil stands alone in the middle. Long leaves that are pointed and curved look like slim green swords protecting the white blossoms.

Spider lilies like warm places to grow, and you see many in southern gardens. But if you live where it's cold in winter, you can grow them in a greenhouse. Just plant some seeds or some pieces of bulb. Be sure to plant in a large pot or small tub, because the new bulbs grow to be very large. Give them plenty of water and your lovely white "spiders" will hang around a long time.

SPIDER LILY
Hymenocallis occidentalis

ANTHER   A sac at the end of a stamen. Anthers contain pollen.

BULB   An onion-shaped underground stem with layers of leaves that store a plant's food. Bulbs live year after year.

CAPSULE   A seed or spore case that breaks apart when seeds or spores are ripe.

CATKIN   A long, fingerlike cluster of small flowers, usually gray or yellow/green. Some catkins produce pollen; others produce seeds.

CORM   Like bulbs, except they are solid instead of being made of layers of leaves and they live only one growing season.

FERTILIZATION   What happens in a plant when pollen and egg cells unite. Fertilization makes it possible for a plant to produce seeds.

NECTAR   Sweet liquid in many flowers. It is usually at the flower's base. Insects gather pollen on their bodies as they feed on or collect the nectar. They carry the pollen to another flower, which may help to fertilize the plant.

OVARY   The part of a plant that holds egg cells. It is at the bottom of a pistil. (See pollen)

PETAL   The bright, colored part of most flowers. The petals' colors (and often the smell) attract birds and insects, which often help pollinate the flower.

PISTIL   The female part of a flower. It normally has three parts: stigma, style and ovary.

POD   A seed case or fruit of a plant, like a pea pod.

POLLEN	Usually yellow, dust-like grains that form by the thousands in the anthers of flowers. When pollen reaches the stigma of a plant it may grow pollen tubes that go down the style to combine with egg cells in the plant's ovary. This is fertilization, which produces seeds.
RACEME	An elongated cluster of flowers growing on one stem. Each flower has a stalk of its own.
SEED	The part of a plant from which new plants grow. A seed starts to develop in a plant's ovary.
SEPAL	Part of a plant just outside the petals. Sepals are often small and green and protect the flower buds. Sometimes, however, they look just like flower petals.
SPORE	A tiny body that can grow like a seed to make a new plant — such as a fern or moss.
STAMEN	The male part of a flower. Stamens are most often long, thread-like stalks topped by an anther sac, which produces pollen.
STIGMA	A tiny part of a flower at the top of a pistil. Its sticky surface catches pollen grains. The grains grow pollen tubes which travel through the style to the ovary. The pollen fertilizes the ovary's egg cells to produce seeds.
STYLE	A long, slender tube that connects the pollen-catching stigma to the egg-bearing ovary.
TUBER	The thick part of an underground stem. It stores food, normally starch, and it sprouts new plants from its "eyes" (small buds). Potatoes are tubers.

COMMON NAME	SCIENTIFIC NAME	PAGE NO.
Elephant's Ear	*Colocasia esculenta*	10
Foxglove	*Digitalis purpurea*	22
Horsetail	*Equisetum hyemale*	16
Moth Mullein	*Verbascum blattaria*	24
Mouse-ear	*Cerastium vulgatum*	18
Pussy Willow	*Salix discolor*	8
Skunk Cabbage	*Symplocarpus foetidus*	12
Snail Flower	*Phaseolus caracalla*	26
Snake Gourd	*Trichosanthes cucumeroides*	20
Snapdragon	*Antirrhinum majus*	14
Spider Lily	*Hymenocallis occidentalis*	28
Tiger Lily	*Lilium tigrinum*	6